HISTORIC PHOTOS OF
SALT LAKE CITY

TEXT AND CAPTIONS BY JEFF BURBANK

TURNER
PUBLISHING COMPANY
NASHVILLE, TENNESSEE PADUCAH, KENTUCKY

This 1950 photo, taken from the apex of the City and County Building (451 South State Street), shows how the development of downtown Salt Lake City had progressed, with some newer buildings including the University of Utah and Judge Mercy Hospital.

HISTORIC PHOTOS OF
SALT LAKE CITY

Turner Publishing Company
200 4th Avenue North • Suite 950   412 Broadway • P.O. Box 3101
Nashville, Tennessee 37219   Paducah, Kentucky 42002-3101
(615) 255-2665   (270) 443-0121

www.turnerpublishing.com

Historic Photos of Salt Lake City

Library of Congress Control Number: 2007929609

ISBN-13: 978-1-59652-385-2

Printed in the United States of America

08 09 10 11 12 13 14 15—0 9 8 7 6 5 4 3 2 1

CONTENTS

Civil War veterans from Utah pose on the ornate porch of a Salt Lake City home in 1888.

Acknowledgments

This volume, *Historic Photos of Salt Lake City,* is the result of the cooperation and efforts of many individuals, organizations, and corporations. It is with great thanks that we acknowledge the valuable contribution of the following for their generous support:

Library of Congress

National Archives

Special Collections Department, J. Willard Marriott Library, University of Utah

Utah State Historical Society

PREFACE

The founding of Salt Lake City continued a tradition dating back to colonial America, as a group of pilgrims sought to establish a place where members of their religion would be free from persecution for their beliefs. The first settlers in the Salt Lake Valley envisioned a planned community where religion, government, and commerce would intermingle. As new residents, practicing other religions, arrived, the role of the Church of Jesus Christ of Latter-day Saints—sometimes simply called "the Church"—was diminished in government and commerce, and the city became more heterogeneous. Regardless, it still holds a unique place among American cities.

Thousands of historic photographs of this shining city near the Great Salt Lake reside in local and national archives. This book began with the observation that, while those photographs are of great interest to many, they are not easily accessible. It seeks to provide easy access to a valuable, objective look into the history of Salt Lake City, for residents and visitors alike.

The power of photographs is that they are less subjective than words in their treatment of history. Although the photographer can make decisions regarding subject matter and how to capture and present it, photographs do not provide the breadth of interpretation that text does. For this reason, they offer an original, untainted perspective that allows the viewer to interpret and observe.

This project represents countless hours of review and research. The researchers and writer have reviewed thousands of photographs in numerous archives. We greatly appreciate the generous assistance of the individuals and organizations listed in the acknowledgments of this work, without whom this project could not have been completed.

The goal in publishing this work is to provide broader access to this set of extraordinary photographs that seek to inspire, provide perspective, and evoke insight that might assist people who are responsible for determining Salt Lake City's future. In addition, the book seeks to preserve the past with adequate respect and reverence.

With the exception of cropping where necessary and touching up imperfections caused by the damage of time, no other changes have been made. The focus and clarity of many images is limited to the technology and the ability of the photographer at the time they were taken.

The work is divided into eras, beginning with the 1880s and concluding in the 1960s. In each of these sections we have made an effort to capture various aspects of life through our selection of photographs. People, commerce, transportation, infrastructure, religious institutions, and educational institutions have been included to provide a broad perspective.

We encourage readers to reflect as they go walking in Salt Lake City, strolling its broad thoroughfares, its parks, and its neighborhoods. It is the publisher's hope that in utilizing this work, longtime residents will learn something new and that new residents will gain a perspective on where the city has been, so that each can contribute to its future.

This wide shot of downtown Salt Lake City, taken from the roof of the City and County Building on May 27, 1920, shows a maturing town. Buildings pictured here include the Walker Brothers Bank Building, First Security Bank Building, Deseret National Bank Building, Hotel Utah, the Joseph Smith Memorial Building, and the Utah State Capitol. Note evidence of changing times—Fuller Auto Works stands next to the Utah Livery Stable, and motor vehicles are parked behind Coombs & Hagen's carriage shop in the center foreground.

FROM MORMON ENCLAVE TO AMERICAN CITY

(1880–1905)

Salt Lake City's long history tells the story of a community founded as both a spiritual center and a planned city. It evolved into a regional center of free enterprise and modern urban life well before the start of the twentieth century.

The city's origins date to late July 1847, when Brigham Young, president of the Church of Jesus Christ of Latter-day Saints, brought his followers, 147 Mormon pioneers (including three women and two children), to a halt during their journey toward California. They were in the uninhabited Salt Lake Valley, fifteen miles outside the shores of the Great Salt Lake Basin. Young and others liked the promise of its fertile ground, abundant timber, and freshwater streams. They founded the city—which they considered a refuge from religious persecution—on July 24, 1847.

That same year, Orson Pratt, one of the Church's Apostles, began his survey of what was called "Great Salt Lake City," beginning at Temple Square. ("Great" was dropped from the name in 1868.) Young and his Twelve Apostles agreed the city would be laid out in blocks of ten acres, with each block holding eight building lots. Streets would be 132 feet wide, sufficient space to turn around a covered wagon with a four-ox team. The new town progressed quickly. The settlement's population reached 1,700 later that year. Schools were established. The University of Deseret, the first university in the West—then defined as anywhere west of the Missouri River—began there in 1849, followed by the region's first theater. (Young had proposed Deseret, "honeybee" in the Book of Mormon, for the provisional state's name, but that was never recognized by the U.S. Government; today, what began as the University of Deseret is the University of Utah.) By 1850, the length of the city's street grid extended almost four miles out and three miles wide. Ground was broken on the Salt Lake Temple in 1853. The first art school in the West, the Deseret Academy of Art, debuted in 1863. In 1868, Mormon leaders opened the Zion's Cooperative Mercantile Institution, considered the nation's first departmentalized store.

By the 1880s, Salt Lake City was already a major Western city, a seat of regional commerce, a railroad shipping hub, and a base for Utah's mining industry, which extracted silver, lead, gold, and other metals and minerals. In that decade, city leaders turned their attention to modernization and improvement projects, from water main, sewage, electric, and gas systems to street paving and a full-time fire department. In 1889, the city began building an advanced electric streetcar system.

The town had grown well beyond its rural, pioneer roots. Since the 1860s, migration to the growing Mormon capital city produced a multi-ethnic and religiously diverse population—including communities of foreign-born English, Canadians, Germans, Slavs, Italians, Greeks, Africans, Chinese, and Japanese. Labor groups organized employees from mining, public works, crafts, and other sectors. On January 4, 1896, about 15,000 people met at the Mormon Tabernacle Dome downtown to celebrate the statehood of Utah. Its constitution outlawed state-supported religion, polygamy, and discrimination on the basis of race, gender, or religion.

With its varied population, Salt Lake City mirrored much of the rest of the immigrant-rich American landscape of the early 1900s. It adapted to the mounting influence of automobile transport, built skyscrapers and parks, promoted spectator sports, and became linked to the increasingly sophisticated national and regional business markets. In little more than half a century after the first Mormon settlers arrived, Salt Lake City had become known as the largest city in the Intermountain region.

Horse-drawn vehicles line up in downtown Salt Lake City in the early 1880s, outside a wagon factory, Studebaker Brothers Manufacturing. The Midwest-based Studebaker company developed a national reputation for building sturdy wagons, popular for use in mining. In 1902, it would begin producing automobiles.

Merchants stand amid elegant draperies and furniture in the high-ceiling interior of the Zion's Cooperative Mercantile Institution in the late 1880s, the center of business in Utah. It is credited as being the first departmentalized store in the United States. Latter-day Saints leaders established the three-story center on 15 South Main Street in 1868, the year that Salt Lake City removed "Great" from its name.

The outside of the Zion's Cooperative Mercantile Institution as it looked on Main Street in the late 1880s. By then, much of downtown Salt Lake City had been planned and developed with municipal and commercial buildings; compare this image with the one on page 3, shot just a few years earlier. Sanitation, however, was a major concern. Dead work animals and garbage piled up along city streets, and the area lacked a sewer system until the 1890s.

Men in suits and women in white Victorian-style dresses and broad-brimmed hats stand at the 400 block of Main Street to view a parade (likely for the Fourth of July, given the American flag-style bunting on the building) in this photo from a glass plate negative taken by photographer William Edward Hook between 1878 and 1882.

Hook snapped this photo from another spot during the same parade, showing the lengths that some spectators would go—such as a dangerous climb to the top of a utility pole—to watch the parade down Main Street. Others parked their horses and buggies right by the parade route to sit in or stand on.

Railroad service to Salt Lake City was well established by the late 1870s, as seen by this photo of the Denver and Rio Grande Railroad Station about 1880. The nation's rails were joined at Promontory Summit, Utah, on May 10, 1869, but the Union Pacific Railroad's route bypassed Salt Lake City in favor of Ogden. The Utah Central Railroad, owned by the Church of Latter-day Saints, was connected to the Union Pacific line in 1870. With 15,000 people watching, Brigham Young himself pounded in the last spike, which linked Salt Lake City with the rest of the United States by rail.

An engineer looks out the window of the engine of a train stopped at the Denver and Rio Grande Depot about 1880. The railroad shipped ore, including silver, copper, lead, and coal, from area mines in places like Bingham and Park City to Salt Lake City for smelting and processing. The city became a mining capital in the region, greatly expanding its economy and the ethnic diversity of its population.

Not long after establishing the Zion's Cooperative Mercantile Institution's main building in 1868, dealing in clothing and dry goods, a second location opened that sold groceries, farm tools, stoves, and hardware.

A three-story decorative star in honor of Utah's statehood adorned the Dinwoodey Furniture building in 1896.

Laying the capstone of the Mormon Temple and Tabernacle in 1892.

Utah takes its name from the Ute tribe, but other Native Americans including the Bannock, Navaho, and Western Shoshone also lived within its borders.

A choir of men, dressed in dark clothing, and women wearing white pose inside the Mormon Tabernacle during statehood celebrations in 1896. The Church's choir would eventually achieve world renown. Brigham Young asked Joseph Harris Ridges, who grew up near an organ factory in England, to construct an organ for the Tabernacle. At various times, its bellows have been powered manually, by water, and finally by electricity.

Hundreds of aging original Mormon pioneers, among those who founded Salt Lake City, sat for this photo on July 24, 1897, while in town to celebrate the Utah Pioneer Jubilee, commemorating the fiftieth anniversary of the city's founding.

Taken from a double-photo "stereocard" (used in dual magnifying glass viewers of the nineteenth century), this image captures the parade of surviving members of the Handcart Company, marching during the Pioneer Jubilee in Salt Lake City in July 1897. Unable to afford enough ox teams and wagons for Latter-day Saints immigrating to the Utah Territory, the Church provided some 650 carts that could be pulled by hand. Nearly 3,000 believers made the trip from Iowa City, Iowa, this way between 1856 and 1860.

Heber M. Wells (left), the first governor of Utah (1896–1905), waits in the rear of an open carriage with a man identified as Admiral Schley (in top hat, right), in front of the Wallace house at 5 Laurel Street on May 30, 1899. This is almost certainly Winfield Scott Schley, who destroyed the remnants of the Spanish fleet as it fled Santiago Bay on July 4, 1898, during the Spanish-American War. Given the May 30 date, he was probably in town for a Decoration Day (Memorial Day) event.

Street paving work (background) is underway to cover the carriage track–worn, dirt surface of South Temple Street, east of Main Street, in 1902. Buildings along the boulevard included the Alta Club, the Gardo House and Amelia's Palace.

The majestic, cathedral-like Salt Lake City and County Building as it stood in 1902, from the southwest, between the 400 and 500 blocks of South, between State Street and 200 East (today, at 451 S. State Street). Reportedly, it was constructed to rival the Temple's magnificence during tensions between Mormon and non-Mormon residents.

Stagecoaches owned by merchant members of the Zion's Cooperative Mercantile Institution line up outside the department store to deliver goods to customers' homes around 1902.

City workers inspect a maze of crisscrossing streetcar tracks during road construction and paving at the intersection of Main Street and South Temple Street in 1902.

President Theodore Roosevelt, flanked by mounted policemen, rides in a carriage down Main Street during a visit to Salt Lake City around 1902.

During a road improvement project at the intersection of South Temple and State Street in 1903, a man walks with a cane beneath the historic Eagle Gate monument, built by Brigham Young in 1859. The Bransford Apartments building is at right.

Men pose in front of the Zion's Cooperative Mercantile Institution's window. Notice the sign proclaims "Holiness for the Lord." Religion permeated every aspect of community life including commerce in Salt Lake City's early history, which ultimately led to growing tension as increasing numbers of non-Mormons settled there.

A newsboy hawks papers while another lad sells American ice cream from a cart on bustling Commercial Street (34 East, between 100 and 200 South), which included the American Hotel (baths 15 cents) and Restaurant, the Palace Cafe, Johnson's Tavern (right side, halfway down the block), and Yee Lee's Laundry. A sign in the alley proclaims, "The New Devil is Coming."

The Main Street storefront of the A. H. Crabbe Co. men's store, owned by Albert H. Crabbe, offers hats for $3.00 in this photo dated June 5, 1905. The Union Dental Co. was up the stairs to the right. In 1916, Crabbe became chairman of the Salt Lake County Commission.

The six-story
Commercial Block
building dominates
the corner at 76
West, 200 South,
on June 19, 1905,
fifteen years after
its construction.
Tenants included
the New York Life
Insurance agency,
attorneys, at least
two dentists (Peake
and Barnett),
and an aurist (ear
specialist) named
Dr. Arthur Douglas.

Employees line the front of the Century Printing Company shop at 167 West Temple Street on November 22, 1905.

A complex of electric lines converge near the Alta Club building, at the intersection of State Street and South Temple, on December 4, 1905. Founded in 1883, its initial members primarily came from the mining industry, but it drew industrial, financial, and social leaders from around the West. It recently underwent a $4.2 million restoration. The building in the background is the University Club.

New Buildings, New Streets, New Faces

(1906–1919)

Already a maturing city, Salt Lake City renewed itself in the first two decades of the twentieth century. Famous original buildings were replaced with modern high rises and low rises. Old cobblestone streets were removed to make way for paved roads to accommodate automobiles and new rail tracks for an expanding electric-powered streetcar system.

Much of this development came from the efforts of Samuel Newhouse, a wealthy copper mining company executive who amassed a large fortune after selling his Utah operation to John D. Rockefeller for $12 million. Newhouse busied himself with erecting some 30 buildings in town, notably the Boston and Newhouse buildings on Exchange and Main streets. But Mormon Church leaders beat him in a competition to construct the city's first great hotel, with the Hotel Utah, in 1911. The Newhouse Hotel followed in 1915. Soon a rivalry developed in the city's business district, with Mormon-owned businesses dominating the northern end and non-Mormon owners the southern blocks near the Newhouse Hotel and the Walker Brothers Bank Building (which for a time was the tallest building in the West). On State Street, the $2.7 million State Capitol Building took shape, designed after the United States Capitol and the state of Maryland's capitol. Catholic, Presbyterian, and Jewish congregations built new institutions in the area of South Temple and East Streets. A reservoir in Parley's Canyon expanded the city's supply of fresh water and improved sanitation when it opened in 1907.

Salt Lake City's population remained largely homogeneous (mainly Anglo-Saxon) in the early part of the century. But with growing employment opportunities, particularly with the Church-owned electric interurban railroad, the Utah Light and Railway Company, the city continued to see an influx of new immigrant populations that created separate ethnic communities with lines of specialty shops and restaurants. Newly arrived Greeks, for instance, moved to an area at Second South between Fourth and Sixth West streets, known as Greektown. Several blocks on First Street South became Japanese Town. Swedish immigrants congregated in Swedetown, on Beck Street.

City residents showed increasing interest in leisure activities, from the silent motion pictures to team sports and racing. The Salt Palace, a stylish, domed building on Ninth Street near Main, was a popular entertainment spot for things like circuses and bicycle races at its outdoor track, until it was destroyed by fire in 1910. The city spent a fortune, $1.5 million, to build a series of parks and playgrounds and to landscape its boulevards. The Salt Lake City Seals minor league baseball team drew even more spectators when it joined the Pacific Coast League and changed its name to the Bees in 1915.

National reforms associated with the Progressive Movement of the early twentieth century, including laws governing public health, food quality, and worker safety, extended to the city as well, with more citizens demanding civic improvements. Air pollution in town, from autos, the railroad, and industry, was a serious problem in the century's second decade. Women's groups, including the Utah Congress of Mothers, the House Wives League and the Ladies Literary Club, campaigned to improve air quality and local literacy. The Board of Health in 1914–15 paid children ten cents for every dead rat or one hundred flies they turned in. The union movement among plumbers, electrical, and other workers expanded—with mixed success—as did the frequency of strikes. In a major stoppage, 5,000 striking workers shut down the Utah Copper Company for months in 1912. World War I, which the United States entered in 1917, dramatically changed Salt Lake City's economy and culture. Utah mines and smelters benefited from the demand for raw materials for military hardware. This period also saw creation of a regulated red-light district to keep prostitutes away from downtown; city government contracted with the madam Dora B. Topham to run a complex of bordellos.

By the 1920s, the Progressive Movement had subsided, but its reforms changed Salt Lake City. Its commission government took action to solve local problems and enhance civic life, and its neutrality helped to quell the city's decades-long political clash between Mormons and non-Mormons.

In the midst of a clothing drive for the refugees of the April 18 earthquake that destroyed much of San Francisco, California, a crowd of men gathered on the sidewalk between the Herald Building and three trucks owned by the Redman Van and Storage Company on Main Street between 100 South and 200 South, April 26, 1906. The Redman company burned down in 1907 and later relocated to 400 West, where it added a fireproof storage facility.

A horse team is hitched to a wagon carrying an Adams Electric Drill, sold by the Salt Lake Hardware Co., at 42–52 West 200 South, May 17, 1906.

A bicyclist in shorts and a man in a suit and hat, astride a motor-powered bike, pose at the Salt Palace on 900 South, between Main and State streets, July 16, 1906.

Patches of snow cover the ground in this bird's-eye view of Salt Lake City, taken in 1907 from on top of the City and County Building, between 400 and 500 South and State Street and 200 East.

People wait at the corner to cross while streetcars drive by during a busy day on Main Street, north of 200 South, about 1907. The tall Scott Building to the left housed the King Hardware and Stove Company. Smith Drug stands at the right corner, with signs down the street for the Salt Lake City car agent, the American Shoe Shine Parlor, and Meredith's Trunks.

The Davis Shoe Company, advertising "Money Back Shoes," attracted a large crowd for Buster Brown brand footwear at 236 South Main Street, on May 17, 1907. To the right is the J. H. Leyson Company jewelry store.

Small carriages line the north side of 200 South Street, west of Main Street, in 1907. A banner on the Cullen Hotel at left announces a complete remodeling has been completed. The hotel stands between the Chesapeake Cafe (foreground) and a billiard hall. The wagon in front of Chesapeake Cafe belongs to John Holley & Co., a wholesaler of butter, eggs, cheese, and poultry, who was probably making a delivery to the cafe.

Men working for Patrick (P. J.) Moran Contractor, Inc., remove old cobblestones and paving while reconstructing streetcar rails at the intersection of Main Street and 200 South in 1907.

The interior framing of the Boston and Newhouse buildings is shown here during the simultaneous construction of the twin structures at the intersection of Exchange Place and Main Street, between 300 South and 400 South, on March 14, 1908.

Men and boys stand on a downtown cobblestone street to watch a man behind the wheel of a single-seat Studebaker car, apparently used for racing, on August 7, 1908.

This bird's-eye shot from atop the City and County Building shows views of Washington Square, the Boston and Newhouse buildings, and Temple Square in 1908. The triple-arch entrance to the Elite Theatre stands in the center foreground. A sign for I X L Furniture Co. on the newly constructed P. A. Sorensen building (center) advertises, "You furnish the girl, we'll furnish the house."

The intersection of Main Street and 300 South, to the northwest, as it looked during a street-paving project in 1908.

An early automobile, decorated to serve as a float promoting the phonograph store during the United Commercial Travelers of America parade, sits at 327–329 Main Street on June 18, 1908.

Main Street to the north was shot from the roof of the Boston Building in 1908. This is a bird's-eye view of the corner shown on page 44.

Workers from the Hamlin Paint Company give the facade of the Castle Hall Building at 261 South Main Street a new paint job on October 17, 1908. Madam Elon Lavera Snyder, "The Gifted Palmist, Psychic, and Card Reader," advertises her services on a large sign near several smaller ones for doctors.

Signs outside the Castle Building advertise a stone treatment "Impervia," used to prevent discoloring due to weather and "canine nuisance," during the building's renovation, October 24, 1908. Notice the sign for Madam Snyder that was photographed above the Van Noy Apartments sign a week earlier is gone.

Slats of wood protrude over the sidewalk, amid makeshift advertising signs, during construction of the Lyceum Theater at 271 25th Street, on January 9, 1909. The poster to left advertises a play that opened in the city the previous month, on December 20.

The Colonial Theater, 144 West 100 South Street, beside B. F. Ott Drug Co., proudly announced a matinee performance of "Shore Acres," starring Archie Boyd on February 6, 1909. Billed as "The Greatest Ladies and Childrens Play Ever Written," the popular show was in its fifteenth year on the American stage. The Will Rees Plumbing Co. was installing heating and plumbing in the building; hopefully, the heating was functional on this snowy day.

Road builders, employed by contractor Patrick "P. J." Moran, remove original cobblestones while paving the east side of Main Street, north of 200 South, outside the Tribune Building, about 1909.

Workers pose beside a line of horse-drawn delivery wagons at the ready outside the American Linen Supply at 130–138 West 100 South on February 20, 1909.

The Hotel Bungalow/ Bungalow Theatre building, 251 South State Street offered patrons both an evening of entertainment and a place to stay overnight, April 14, 1909. *La Tosca*, advertised on the rooftop marquee, may have been the touring play or the French movie version starring Sarah Bernhardt, which was released that year. Note the cracked and damaged surface of street.

Sawhorses line the center of Main Street, south of Temple, during another paving project by P. J. Moran, outside the Zion's Cooperative Mercantile Institution (at left), about 1909. The Salt Lake Security and Trust Company and the Constitution Building are also pictured. The city was in the midst of an extensive effort to macadamize its streets and plant "parks" in the medians.

A sign advertising Cuban cigars fronts the College Inn and Cafe, 237 Main Street, on April 21, 1909. At left is the Utah Savings and Trust Company, and at right, Reagan's Bar and the Delmar Lunch Room.

A steamroller rumbles along the curb of Main Street, north of 300 South, with streetcars
in the distance about 1909. Among the structures pictured are the Scott Building and the
McCornick Block.

Dozens of young military cadets gather outside the YMCA Building (center) during the Commercial Club's building campaign, at the southeast corner intersection of 100 South and State streets, May 12, 1909. The Utah Independent Telephone Company building is at left.

A large throng showed up to watch a crane lower the cornerstone of the new Commercial Club Building at 34 Exchange Place on July 5, 1909. The image also shows parts of the Boston Building (center) and post office (in background, with flags, right).

The majestic Boston Building, eleven floors high, as it looked on July 16, 1909. Its rounded corner was on the northeast corner of Exchange Place and Main Street.

Streetcar tracks and overhead electrical lines lead to the Oregon Short Line Railroad Depot, which was still under construction when this picture was taken on July 29, 1909, at the west end of South Temple, 300 West (today at 400 West). The line was part of the Union Pacific Railroad. Its galvanized iron cornice and roofing were manufactured by J. A. Johnson of Salt Lake City.

Building contractor P. J. Moran's crew removes cobblestones onto wagons during street reconstruction and paving on the west side of Main Street and 200 South, about 1909.

Paving projects in downtown Salt Lake City were done to facilitate the emerging automobile, like this classic model parked outside D. J. Watts' barbershop at 17 West South Temple, on July 31, 1909.

Sword-wielding high school students front a musical band of their fellow cadets during a parade down Main Street, south of 200 South, on August 24, 1909.

Two horses, one hitched to a delivery wagon, wait outside the Clayton-Daynes Music Company, which sold a variety of instruments, large and small, as well as phonographs, at 17 West South Temple on September 23, 1909.

A barbershop (advertising baths for 15 cents), plus a hotel (rooms available for 25, 35 or 50 cents a night), a saloon, and pool parlor were all part of this corner of Commercial Street, at 34 East between 100 South and 200 South, on September 28, 1909. A few doors down, the Salvation Army "Workingmans Hotel" offered bed and bath for just 10 cents.

A row of soldiers and an officer stand at attention opposite a group of bystanders, in anticipation of a parade marking a visit by President William Howard Taft on September 25, 1909.

Two lines of military cadets wait along a parade route for a carriage transporting President Taft, September 25, 1909.

Rows of carriages stand inside the corridor between the twin modern buildings, Boston (left) and Newhouse (right), facing east on Exchange Place, September 30, 1909.

A bicycle is parked in front of the Intermountain Electric Company, between horse-drawn vehicles at 13 South Main Street, on November 6, 1909. Cannon Brothers Architects and Engineers were upstairs. Next door on the left, at Number 11, was the George Q. Cannon Association, Real Estate and Brokerage, ("We sell the Earth").

Automobile passengers pose in front of the Colonial Theater at 144 West 100 South, which was presenting the popular musical comedy play *The Time, the Place, and the Girl*, on November 7, 1909. When the play was made into a movie twenty years later, it starred Betty Compson of Beaver, Utah, who attended high school in Salt Lake City.

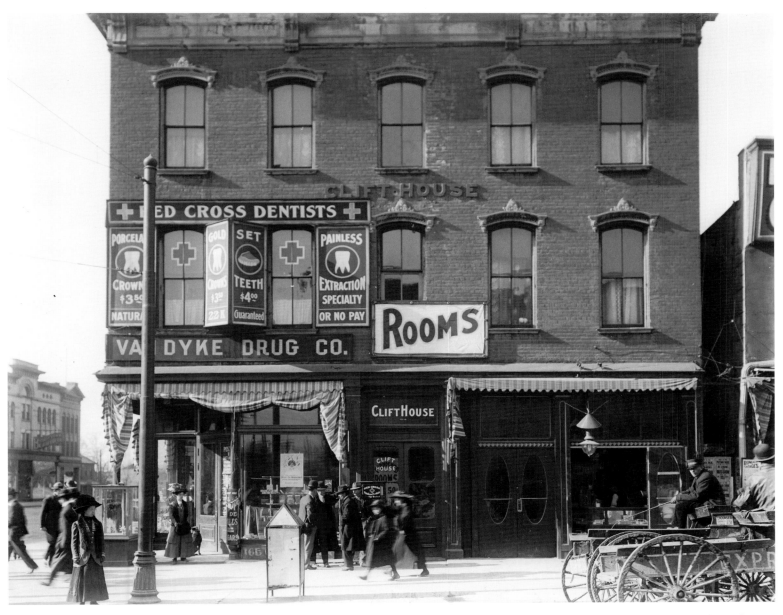

The three-story Clift House hotel shared its location at 280 South Main Street with the Red Cross Dentist and the Van Dyke Drug Co., November 27, 1909.

The Lion House (center), beside the Beehive House (left), owned by the Church of Jesus Christ of Latter-day Saints, between Main Street and State Street, south of Temple, about 1910.

Horses and wagons stand in the main business district of the mining town of Bingham, Utah, a few miles southwest of Salt Lake City, about 1910. The town was consumed by expanded mining operations in the 1970s.

A rider, with umbrella, sits inside a stationary buggy on Salt Lake City's Main Street about 1910.

Three horses were needed to pull a wagon used by the Redman Van & Storage Company at 113–117 South West Temple in 1910. Its advertising slogan, "Its your move," was cleverly painted on a pattern resembling a chess board. Note the three-digit phone number; today, 555 is the standard telephone prefix used in films and television shows, because it isn't assigned within the United States.

Early electric-powered automobiles of the Taxicab and Automobile Company, with uniformed drivers, were ready for hire (via telephone number 1598) on January 25, 1910. The location was on Eagle Block, between 200 and 300 South, West Temple, shared by Crismon & Nichols Assayers, the Big 4 Advertising Company, and an enormous wall side advertisement painted by the Utah Billposting Co., touting Henry George brand 5-cent cigars.

A group of men and a boy in a cap pose with a Buick from the Randall-Dodd Auto Company, outside 229 South Main Street, where William A. Stickney Cigar Company and Hulbert Brothers Trunk Manufacturers were located, February 21, 1910.

Men and youths band together to witness a historic occasion—placement of the final streetcar pole to complete the citywide electric transit system, at the intersection of Main Street and 200 South, near the Walker Brothers Bank Building (center), Park's Jewelry Store (center right), and the Scott Building (right), about 1910.

Main Street, north of 200 South, with the Herald Building and the McCornick Block, about 1910.
Businesses included Mehesy Furs (left center), Margells Bros. Toys, Books and Stationery (next to last
building on left), and Salt Lake Medical (right center), as well as street-vendors' carts.

American flags and flag-colored decorations adorn the front of the monument honoring Brigham Young and the pioneers, on Temple Square at the intersection of South Temple and Main Street, about 1910.

A sign warns "Beware of Pickpockets" during the spring General Conference on Temple Square, at 50 West South Temple near the Bureau of Information Office, on April 4, 1910. The Deseret News Building is at right.

A right-side driver with a youngster sit inside a Buick car aimed toward the camera outside the Randall-Dodd Auto Company, 231 South State Street, on April 14, 1910. The cross on the grill may have been part of a promotion for the Red Cross organization or for the city's Red Cross Drugstore.

82

Three men pause while working to convert an automobile into a vehicle to
carry small groups of tourists, April 17, 1910.

Telephone and streetcar lines and poles run end to end through this general shot of 200 South, west of Main Street, also known as Commercial Block, about 1910. A sign on the corner building informs passersby that J. P. Paulson of 170 & 174 "W. 2nd S. St." provided the fixtures used in that bank.

The Salt Lake City Fire Department's Engine House 3, at 1131 East 1200 South, is decorated with American flag bunting and eagle posters about 1910. The building also served as a substation for the city police department.

The combined
Constitution and
Security Trust Buildings
at 34 South Main Street
dominate this picture,
taken on April 19, 1910.
Small businesses seen
here include the Cutler
Brothers investment
company, the Salt Lake
Glass & Paint Company,
J. Burrows & Company,
and Heber J. Grant.
Beyond the horse's head
is a florist's kiosk, and
a photographer's studio
occupies the small
building at far left.

White-capped, uniformed union members prepare to walk in the annual Labor Day Parade, September 5, 1910.

Flowers, ice cream, fruits, toiletries, and cut-rate drugs were among wares available at Brice's State Pharmacy, a corner store at 18 South Main Street, on October 21, 1910.

This bird's-eye view of a well-developed downtown Salt Lake City was shot from the City and County building, facing northwest, on January 10, 1911. Among the prominent buildings pictured are the Moxum Hotel, the Boston and Newhouse buildings on Exchange Place, and the Judge and Kearns buildings.

A gardener is nearly obscured by the flower bushes growing inside this elongated greenhouse owned by the Salt Lake Floral Company at 1950 South State Street, March 31, 1911.

With aviation still in its infancy, onlookers at Saltair, a resort in Salt Lake County, stand to watch a demonstration of aircraft, as an automobile (right) whizzes by, April 6, 1911.

During the Salt Lake City *Tribune's* "Buy a paper to support the Humane Society fund" promotion, some actors and actresses helped sell papers in front of the Tribune Building, on Progress Block, 141–153 South Main Street, about 1911. Humane societies in that era generally aided needy, often orphaned, children, rather than animals.

Military equipment is loaded onto this covered wagon, led by four horses and its soldier driver, at Fort Douglas, a few miles east of Salt Lake City, on April 7, 1911.

In this promotional shot taken on May 28, 1911, men sit on early-model motorcycles at the Bicycle Supply Company, 64 West 300 South, which is advertising an upcoming race at the Salt Palace. Two other businesses in the picture are the Hubbard Investment Company (left) and H. E. Giers and Company (selling furniture, at right).

Burros are employed to hold signs advertising the Alford Brothers Company, a clothing store at 15 West 200 South, on August 11, 1911. A man dressed as a mining prospector (center) apparently is meant to accompany the animals. Each sign contains the motto, "Go West Young Man," popularized by the nineteenth-century journalist Horace Greeley, publisher of the New York *Tribune*.

A manned balloon floats over this scene of Main Street, which includes the White House Hotel, at right, on the block of 200 South, September 6, 1911.

The Star Bargain store attracts lines of customers for its "Fire, Smoke and Water Sale" of clothing held inside Daniel's Theater at 253 South State Street, September 7, 1911.

The Brigham Young Trust Company Building as it stood at 27–39 Commercial Street on September 28, 1911.

President William Howard Taft, on a platform decorated with flags and plants, gestures during an address at the Utah State Fair Grounds during an official visit on October 5, 1911. Taft served one term, from 1909 to 1913.

A crowd of men wait for the doors to open outside the A. H. Crabbe men's clothing store, at 220 South Main Street, on Harkins Block, on May 11, 1912, during a sale to raise $15,000 in fifteen days. Three newsboys (foreground) apparently were taking the opportunity to sell papers.

The University of Utah men's baseball team and its managers pose with grandstands behind them, on the home field on the east end of 200 South at Presidents Circle (1400 East), May 23, 1912.

On Pioneer Day, July 24, 1912, honoring the original Mormon pioneers who settled Salt Lake City in 1847, the Armour and Company meat store used vines and bunting to decorate its horse-pulled float for the upcoming parade, shown here at Liberty Park (currently 922 South 700 East).

Covered cars from the Campbell Auto Company form a procession at Liberty Park along the crowded route of the Pioneer Day parade, on July 24, 1912.

Two men in a packed auto stopped in Salt Lake City at the Bertram Motor Supply Company, 249–251 South State Street, on September 21, 1912, while on a marathon drive from San Francisco to New York City promoting the future Panama-Pacific Exposition.

The Republican Party festooned its headquarters at the Merchants Bank building, 227 Main Street, with American flags and fabric decorations, October 2, 1912, in preparation for the upcoming presidential election. Their man, incumbent William Taft, who had visited Salt Lake City the year before, lost to Democrat Woodrow Wilson.

The arrowhead-shaped arch of the Eagle Gate Monument (left) is seen beside the Bransford Apartment House and intersecting streetcar power lines at South Temple and State Street, October 21, 1912. Eagle Gate was first built in 1859 to mark the entrance to Brigham Young's property at the mouth of City Creek Canyon. It has been replaced several times.

Large rooftop signs on the Auerbach Building tout the multi-floored department store on the northeast corner of State Street and Broadway as "Utah's Most Popular," November 16, 1912.

Dental services and men's clothes were available on the second floor of the Walker Brothers Bank Building at 200 South and Main Street, November 22, 1912.

Horses drag a plow owned by the Cooperative Wagon and Machine Company while grading a strip of ground in Salt Lake County, as adults, children and their pets look on, May 20, 1913. The grading may have been for extension of the Bamberger Intercity Railway, which renamed this area Cleverly Crossing in 1920.

Advanced park and landscaping work, including grass, flowers and paths, are evident along the center of a residential area on 1200 East, from South Temple, on June 6, 1913. Mayor Ezra Thompson had announced a city-wide beautification effort, which included park-like medians, in April 1906.

In Sandy (now a Salt Lake City suburb), residents stand outside the Oldham, Powell and Company store below a sign that advertises the Bywater Fire Extinguisher and Fire Department Supply Company and welcomes visiting union firemen, August 21, 1913.

On Capitol Hill at the Utah State Capitol, dignitaries pose amid American flags during a ceremony marking the laying of the statehouse building's cornerstone, on April 4, 1914. Salt Lake City has always been Utah's territorial and state capital, with the exception of 1851–56, when the town of Fillmore was the legal capital.

How many spools? That's what the Shipler Studios, a commercial photography company at 151 South Main Street, asked of passersby about a pile of film spools in its front window, for a contest held July 1–August 15, 1914. The winner was to receive a trip to Yellowstone National Park from the company "at our expense." This image was taken on July 10.

Park's Jewelry Store, with its rooftop and painted wall signs, was the main tenant of the five-story Boyd Park Building (center), at 170 South Main Street, September 21, 1914.

Street resurfacing by contractor P. J. Moran on Main Street doesn't seem to stop activity among streetcars, autos and wagons at 200 South and Main. This bird's-eye view includes the corner high-rise Walker Brothers Bank Building at 175 Main Street, about 1914.

Scaffolding and construction cranes jut out beside the planned rotunda during
construction of the Utah State Capitol building, January 15, 1915.

Dressed in earlier-period costumes, students of East High School dance during a festival at the school, at 1300 East, between 800 South and 900 South, on March 9, 1915.

Men pose inside automobiles in a promotional picture for the Bettilyon Home
Builders Company, at 340–342 Main Street, on March 19, 1915.

A pair of travelers at an auto touring company on an unidentified Salt Lake City street have packed their car and are ready to go, June 21, 1915.

An "Official Guide Post Truck" owned by the B. F. Goodrich tire company is parked by the firm's Salt Lake City location, 128 South State Street, next to two men astride an early motorcycle, on September 15, 1915.

Announcements tacked up outside the Central Coal & Coke Company draw the attention of pedestrians at 131 South Main Street on November 18, 1915.

Snowfall provides a scenic, late-winter view of the Salt Lake City and County
Building, between 400 and 500 South, on March 24, 1916.

Another sign of progress comes to Main Street with the addition of this tall, electric lamp post, installed by the Utah Power and Light Company, north of 100 South, October 5, 1916.

A temporary archway, known as the No-Ni-Shee Arch, was built near the intersection of Main and South Temple streets for the Wizard of the Wasatch celebration, September 21, 1916. The arch was dedicated to No-Ni-Shee, the name of a mythical Native American "salt princess," whose salt-filled tears were believed to have made the Great Salt Lake. During the 1916 celebration, salt water was sprayed on the arch and it later crystallized on Main Street.

Modern, mechanized equipment combined with old-fashioned hand labor to pave streets for automobiles. This photo was taken at 1300 East Street, October 9, 1916.

In a unique bit of staging, the Swanson Theater Company performs a play on the main floor while the audience views the actors from the balcony, at 241–243 South Main Street, November 18, 1916.

Joseph Simons, a grocer, stands next to a Kelly-Springfield delivery truck, filled with hay bales outside the 10th Ward cash grocery, hay, grain, and coal store, 424 South East, on January 19, 1917.

With electric lights overhead, men sit at study tables inside the main reading room of the Salt Lake City Free Public Library (currently the Hansen Planetarium) at 15 South State Street, March 7, 1917.

A couple of men in business suits stand next to a delivery truck for the Clover Dairy, near the New York Building, on what was Post Office Park (present-day Market Street), at 340 South, between Main and Temple streets, May 27, 1917. The Boston Building can be seen in the distance (center right).

Several men and a dog pose beside a packed automobile in front of the Chevrolet Motor Company dealership at 141–143 East 100 South, June 28, 1917.

The Standard Fuel Company boasted of owning a "Pierce Arrow 5 Ton" truck to haul coal to customers for heating and cooking. The vehicle was parked outside the Tom Botterill Automobile Company, 36–42 South State Street, on August 15, 1917.

Amid thick drifts of snow, a large shipment of bicycles in narrow boxes sits outside the Charles A. Fowler store at 112 West 200 South on January 17, 1918. The picture also shows other businesses in the building to the right: the Utah Machinery Company, Lodge Pool Room and Eber W. Hall Undertaker, Funeral Director and Embalmer.

An auto traffic light pole fits into the center of intersecting street rail tracks outside the Auerbach Building, on the northeast corner of State Street and Broadway, May 11, 1918.

Automobiles show a greater presence downtown in this shot of 200 South, east from West Temple toward Main Street, taken on May 11, 1918. The sign of the Orpheum Theater (renamed the Capitol Theater in 1927) is at right, and farther down the street is the Walker Brothers Bank Building.

This group of young boys posed for a photograph on an early model bus near the Gardner and Adams Company's store, at 138–140 South Main Street, July 22, 1918.

The cylindrical Anderson Tower, shown here with an automobile parked in front on May 14, 1919, was built in 1884 by Robert R. Anderson, who thought that tourists might pay to go to the top to see its view of Salt Lake City. The venture didn't make money, but the Anderson tower remained for decades at A Street, 5th Avenue, until it was torn down in 1932.

THE DEPRESSION STALLS PUBLIC IMPROVEMENTS

(1920–1939)

In the 1920s, concern over the use of political connections and patronage brought further refinements to the progressive approach of professional management of Salt Lake City's government. The decade began with the end of a political scandal over what some (represented by the Civic Betterment Union) believed was a lack of enforcement of laws against prostitution and other vice in the city. Mayor W. Mont Ferry, elected in 1915, angrily rejected the Union's efforts, as did the chief of police and officials appointed by Ferry. Betterment Union supporters were frustrated until 1920, when the new mayor, E. A. Bock, a one-time city auditor, resigned after admitting he embezzled city funds. Reformers formed a majority when the city appointed two of them to the governing Commission, including one as mayor, C. Clarence Nelson. However, Nelson would prove to be more of a centrist in the 1920s, and residents, though agreeable to public improvements, remained divided on how to enforce moral reforms.

Government reforms continued in the early 1920s when the state, to reduce political influences, put a civil service commission in charge of hiring and promoting police and fire personnel. The state also permitted Salt Lake City in 1925 to institute zoning laws to regulate the location of new construction. The city commission used its powers to withhold business licenses from those guilty of illegal gambling, liquor sales during Prohibition and other vices. Commissioners, who previously included members who doubled as businessmen, now worked full time as town overseers. By the late 1920s, auto traffic congestion prompted the city to change parking on its paved streets from parallel to diagonal. Salt Lake City became the first municipality anywhere to replace its public trolleys, which ran on rails, with tire-wheel buses, an advance that attracted international attention. In the 1930s, the city accomplished a similar feat—it introduced the first public buses with engines in the rear.

Policies to reduce air pollution from factories and railroad engines proved largely successful in the 1920s, although smoke from home heating continued to foul the city's air. Better water and sewage systems and vaccinations prevented most diseases in the 1920s, except for a wave of diphtheria from 1925 to 1927 that killed seventeen people, one of the world's worst fatal outbreaks of the disease.

By 1930, a census showed that the city of 140,000 was still predominantly made up of people originally from northwestern Europe. Even the 29 percent of city residents who were foreign born had immigrated from England, Scandinavia, Germany, Switzerland, or the Netherlands. The city maintained its status as the dominant metropolis of the Intermountain West. It now had seventy-five hotels. Its downtown, a center for banking and product distribution, had high-rise office buildings, major department stores, and housed the capital of the Church.

When the national Depression hit in the early 1930s, Utah ended up worse off than most states. The state's unemployment rate rose to 35 percent, while the U.S. jobless rate peaked at 25 percent. In Salt Lake City, unemployed walked the streets and stood in the cold in bread lines in front of charity-run soup kitchens. Some 12,000 families had to seek government relief. Federal programs such as the Works Progress Administration employed thousands of residents in public works jobs into the 1940s. But economic recovery started to appear in the mid-1930s. In 1936, the Church instituted the Church Security Plan, or the Welfare Plan, a work and relief project that removed 15,000 Church members from federal programs.

In the midst of the economic downturn of the 1930s, Salt Lake City nonetheless benefited from an increase in tourism as more people traveled by car. The top visitor destinations were Temple Square downtown and nearby ski resorts. In 1939, more than 400,000 people, a record, visited the city. Also that year, after a major bribery scandal in 1938 involving the city's mayor and police chief, voters elected celebrity auto racer Ab Jenkins mayor in a close election. Far more significant changes were on the horizon for the city, with the coming world war.

General John J. "Black Jack" Pershing, the venerated commander-in-chief of the U.S. Army Expeditionary Force during World War I, stands (facing camera) inside a flag-draped auto as a crowd watches in front of the Utah Hotel at 15 East South Temple, on January 16, 1920. At the time, Pershing (1860–1948), was still in service. Congress named him General of the Armies, a permanent rank that previously had been accorded only to George Washington, and that posthumously.

Large, sculpted heads of Zeus protrude from the facade at the entrance of the Casino Theater at 132 South State Street. On February 3, 1920, it was advertising live vaudeville acts and the movie *What Would You Do,* starring Madlaine Traverse in a role that required her to wear a Boer woman's clothes and not wash her face for several days during filming.

The Utah State Capitol can be seen in the distance in this view of State Street
to the north, February 16, 1920.

Harry Pantelakis, a Greek-American baker, smokes a cigar while posing on the running board of the delivery truck for his Athens Bakery, located at 562 W. 2nd Street South, about 1920.

A circus sideshow, with various animal acts and a pair of carnival barkers on podiums, stands ready for paying customers, in the area north of 400 South, on April 26, 1920.

Two employees of the Pyke-Druehl Company, at 154 West 200 South, look over an example of advanced business technology——a Burroughs adding machine——on April 27, 1920.

The Rogers Amusement Company put on a carnival, with a small Ferris wheel and sideshow (background left) north of 400 South, east of State Street, April 28, 1920. The City and County Building is in view at far left. One booth advertises J. G. McDonald chocolates, while another—not yet completed—promotes the American Legion organization representing military veterans. Salt Lake City's Service Star Legion (also called the War Mothers) was the first of the SSL groups in America. They improved and supported Memory Grove Park and Memorial House.

With flags hanging over his head, President Woodrow Wilson, tipping his hat to onlookers, stands inside an open car in a parade given in his honor downtown about 1920. Wilson served as president from 1913 to 1921.

Empty stools line the shiny counter of the soda fountain inside the Willes-Horne Drug store at 8 South Main Street, on May 24, 1920.

A crowd gathers to watch a devastating fire that swept through a stadium grandstand in Salt Lake City about 1920.

Two men stand beside a Ford Coupe in the street by the Ford dealership and showroom operated by the
Beveridge Motor Company, 309–315 East Broadway, May 25, 1920.

Empty display signs top the Auerbach Building in this view of the northeast corner of State Street and Broadway, on May 26, 1920.

The newly built Keith O'Brien Building, with a distinctive sign bearing the owner's initials, rules over both sides of the southwest corner of State Street and 300 South, June 10, 1920.

Four children in paper hats and carrying flags dance to a record playing on an early portable phonograph, behind the Thompson mansion at 529 East South Temple, August 13, 1920.

Three men representing the Botterill Auto Company pose with a Dodge model automobile outside the B. F. Goodrich tire company store at 50 East 400 South, August 19, 1920. The "one half million" on the car door may refer to the total number of Dodge autos sold in the United States at the time. The Thomas Botterill auto dealership company, which sold cars in Salt Lake City, was based in Denver.

The soda fountain and well-stocked shelves and display counters, some with cutout advertisements, inside the 6th Avenue Drug store at 402 6th Street, August 27, 1920. Above the candy counter (right background), a Sweets Salt Lake Chocolates ad hangs beside one for Cracker Jacks.

The Old Walker Bank Building, amid other businesses and intersecting streetcar lines, are seen in this general view of 200 South, taken on November 30, 1920.

The Clift Building as it looked on Main Street and 300 South on December 1, 1920.

A Salt Lake & Utah electric interurban railroad engine pulls a couple of cars through an area of Salt Lake City, 1920s.

The Paris Millinery Company building (right) stands out in this view down 300 South, with the 300 South Pantages Theater (center right) followed by the Keith O'Brien Building, February 17, 1921.

Proud workers pose with boxes of products piled to capacity on this truck, owned by the Berriju Company, at 152–154 East South Street, on May 21, 1921.

Bundles of clothing, one with a child perched atop it, were collected by Salt Lake City residents to send to Japan to help victims of the Great Kanto Earthquake, a massive quake that occurred there on September 1, 1923.

The train engine is fired up on July 1, 1920, to carry members of the Benevolent & Protective Order of Elks and their wives to the organization's national convention in Chicago.

Workers stand at the soda fountain inside of the Zion's Cooperative Mercantile Institution at 15 South Main
Street in the 1920s. By then, the department store was almost a half-century old.

Members of a Japanese-American baseball team (with team symbol "S") pose with a catcher's mitt and some fanned bats in 1929. They are, from left to right, Jack Chiba, Terry Adachi, Bob Okuda, S. Tatai, Koh Tatai, the manager identified as Mr. Yoshida, Hisao Chiba, Frank Kido and Mas Nakamoto.

In this wide-angle shot, people relax beneath shade trees as others inspect the shops and attractions at a recreational fairway known as the Lagoon, about 1930.

On the Union Pacific Railroad depot's platform, at the west end of South Temple Street, rail passengers stand for this picture with the Gold Coast Limited commuter train, about 1930.

The proprietor of Lingo's Grocery, specializing in Greek-style food, at 126 West and 2nd south, about 1930.

Buses—or "stages" as they were still called—are parked outside and in the terminal of the Pickwick Stages System. Mechanics are lined at left and uniformed drivers are at right, with what appear to be managers and office staff, at 27 North West Temple, about 1931.

Salt Lake City's minor league baseball team (in white uniforms, left) lines the first base side of their home field, opposite the team from Boise, Idaho, about 1935. An announcer is sitting in a box hanging over the grandstands, which are full of spectators.

A cloud-filled sky looms over a series of small houses and lines of trees in this broad view of the southern section of the Salt Lake Valley, looking east, about 1930.

The famous film comedians the Marx Brothers at the Union Pacific depot, April 10, 1935. They were likely in town for a live theater performance; their next film, *Night at the Opera,* would be released later that year.

Daredevil auto driver Ab Jenkins (right) stands with "Mr. Wilkinson," owner of the Wilkinson Motor Company, next to a 1936 Cord model car at Wilkinson's auto store at 155 East Social Hall Avenue, September 2, 1936. Jenkins became famous for setting automobile speed records driving on the Bonneville Salt Flats in Utah, from 1932 all the way to 1956, in his vehicle, the *Mormon Meteor III*. Jenkins was Salt Lake City's mayor from 1940 to 1943.

On a snow-covered Temple Square, the Mormon Tabernacle auditorium, with its board dome, as it appeared in this northwesterly view, February 20, 1937.

A Salt Lake City streetcar, Bamberger Electric #354, running on a line powered by 750 volts, waits to return to service, March 9, 1938.

Suburban Growth and Presidential Visits

(1940–1968)

As it entered the 1940s, Salt Lake City still suffered from the effects of the Depression, with thousands of workers remaining in federal New Deal jobs. Locals receiving paychecks from the Works Progress Administration worked on a variety of public improvement projects, such as repairing streets and building sewers, but as was true for the rest of the country, the city's economy did not recover fully until thousands were put to work in the local defense industry after America entered World War II.

The war brought a sudden surge in local employment and per capita income. In 1942, with the country fighting in Europe and the Pacific, defense-related federal spending created 12,000 jobs, and by 1943, nearly 50,000 new jobs. Business for city merchants also soared as most of the U.S. military stationed in Utah, about 60,000 recruits, lived near the city. Fort Douglas served as the new base for the U.S. Army's Ninth Corps Area Service Command. Government spending on military industries led to the creation of the Remington Small Arms Plant and pumped $20 million into the Utah Oil Refinery. Area factories made radio tubes and smelted copper, aluminum, and tungsten.

Salt Lake City went through the rationing of various products from sugar to gasoline, as well as product shortages and family problems that beset other communities in the war years. With fewer parents at home, juvenile delinquency rose, as did the rate of divorce. The influx of soldiers and defense workers made housing very scarce, and the U.S. government paid to build or repair hundreds of home units for families. However, more city kids joined groups such as the Boy Scouts, and more people attended church services during the war. The difficulties on the home front eased, starting with the war's end in 1945, but Salt Lake City had to ready itself for the post-war years, with fewer benefits from federal spending.

Within several years, private companies had bought many of the former government-funded companies, including the Remington plant, the Geneva Steel plant, and the Utah Oil Refining Company. In fact, in 1950, more than 570 manufacturing plants were said to be located within 25 miles of Salt Lake City. A growth in tourism and major national sporting events, such as downhill skiing, also contributed to the city's post-war economic expansion. Meanwhile, the city's population grew little from the 1950s to early 1960s, as former residents moved out to the suburbs and rural areas. The composition of the city's populace, which reached 189,000 in 1960, shifted, too, as more Mormons left the city than non-Mormons (although Mormons still represented close to half the city's population in the 2000s).

Possibly in part due to the exodus to suburbia, not much was done to improve or expand Salt Lake City's historic downtown in the early post-war years. Only one new large building would be added by 1960, the First Security Bank Building, located at Fourth South and Main Street. It was the first significant development downtown in almost three decades. As more city residents traveled by car following the war, ridership on city public transit declined into the 1960s. The city's system, and other Utah transit systems, eventually became state-funded.

Salt Lake City, along with many American metro areas, experienced inner-city decay in the decades following World War II. Its population declined for a time, falling to 163,000 people in 1980. Still, the downtown area enjoyed a spate of minor building projects in the 1960s. In the 1970s, preservationists sought to block the destruction of important downtown structures in favor of renovating them. Some, like the Zion's Cooperative Mercantile Institute and Hotel Utah, were saved and improved, but many others were demolished. Salt Lake City would excel in the arts in the 1960s and 1970s, earning a reputation as the capital of theater and the performing arts of the Intermountain area. Major developments, the ZCMI Center Mall and Crossroads Mall, transformed Main Street in the mid-1970s. By the 2000s, the city had 178,000 residents, in a metro area populated by 1 million. While the city's economy has shifted from mining and railroads to mainly banking and business services (and tourism from nearby ski resorts), Salt Lake City remains an organic, expanding, and livable city, mindful of its Mormon past and influences and of its variety of cultures, religions, and opinions.

With the Utah State Capitol as an appropriate backdrop, members of the Utah State Highway Patrol's motorcycle squad pose for this picture about 1940.

Automobiles parked in various positions cluster within the open market at 130–150 Pacific Avenue about 1940.

Popular car speedster Ab Jenkins, serving as mayor of Salt Lake City, helps a girl in period dress out of a horse-drawn coach outside the City and County Building, 451 State Street, on November 21, 1941.

The Auerbach Building (center) dominates this wide-angle photo at 300 South
between Main Street and State Street, August 1, 1946.

Well-stocked with Chevy cars and trucks, the Streator Chevrolet dealership is seen in this shot at 465 South Main Street, with the City and County Building at left, June 22, 1948. Civilian car manufacturing had been put on hold during the war, and when peace came, Americans bought vehicles in record numbers.

A large crowd gathered around this flower-covered coffin at 247 West 100 South, on March 21, 1949, was photographed by Ben Terashima, who recorded many images of the city's Japanese-American community.

Discounted goods were to be found in the basement of the Zion's Cooperative Mercantile Institution on Main Street, shown here crowded with patrons in 1949.

The Fred A. Carleson Company, at 535 South Main Street, was a full-service auto center—new cars, used cars (right), and a Chevron gas and service station (left), June 17, 1949.

Twin towers frame the Holy Trinity Greek Church, beside the World War II memorial building at left, late 1940s.

President Harry S. Truman arrived in Salt Lake City in 1952 for a whistle-stop campaign visit to help the candidacy of Democratic Party presidential nominee Adlai Stevenson and running mate John J. Sparkman. Their Republican opponents, General Dwight Eisenhower and Richard Nixon, would win the election later that year.

Heavy traffic speeds through the intersection of 2100 South and 110 East, past storefronts and pedestrians in the Sugar House district, December 1950. The Southeast Theatre was showing *All About Eve,* which would win the Academy Award for Best Picture that year.

Ab Jenkins, in a pith helmet, took a break from speeding cars on the Bonneville Salt Flats to officiate an Independence Day soapbox derby for local boys, July 4, 1951.

The well-attended Days of '47 Parade in 1952 featured this dressed-up Italian-American Civic League float, flying flags of both countries.

Police officers keep watch as President John F. Kennedy reaches to shake a hand at the Utah Hotel, 15 East South Temple, during his visit to Salt Lake City on September 27, 1963—less than two months before his assassination.

Standing behind a lectern with the presidential seal affixed to it, President Kennedy addresses a crowd, with the renowned Mormon Tabernacle Choir behind him inside the Salt Lake Tabernacle, 50 West South Temple, on September 27, 1963.

Recently elected governor Calvin Lewellyn Rampton, a Democrat, speaks in the Utah Supreme Court after his inauguration on January 4, 1965. Rampton would continue in office until 1977.

The Zions First National
Bank and its clock, on a
sunny morning at First
South and Main streets,
August 1968.

Cars of the 1960s are parked outside a brownstone-style building from another era, the Utah Commercial & Savings Bank, at 22 East First South Street, August 1968. As residents moved to the suburbs, downtown entered a period of decline, but in the 1970s, many old buildings were restored.

Notes on the Photographs

These notes, listed by page number, attempt to include all aspects known of the photographs. Each of the photographs is identified by the page number, photograph's title or description, photographer and collection, archive, and call or box number when applicable. Although every attempt was made to collect all available data, in some cases complete data was unavailable due to the age and condition of some of the photographs and records.

II SALT LAKE CITY, NORTH AND EAST
Used by permission, Utah State Historical Society, all rights reserved
39222000703102

VI CIVIL WAR VETERANS
J. Willard Marriott Library
University of Utah
P0104

X DOWNTOWN
Used by permission, Utah State Historical Society, all rights reserved
39222000699426

3 HORSE-DRAWN VEHICLES
Library of Congress
157784pu

4 MERCHANTS STAND AMID ELEGANT DRAPERIES
Library of Congress
157791pu

5 ZION'S COOPERATIVE MERCANTILE INSTITUTION
Library of Congress
157787pu

6 MAIN STREET PARADE
Used by permission, Utah State Historical Society, all rights reserved
44

7 PARADE
Used by permission, Utah State Historical Society, all rights reserved
45

8 D & RG RR STATION
Used by permission, Utah State Historical Society, all rights reserved
03

9 TRAIN AT D & RG RR STATION
Used by permission, Utah State Historical Society, all rights reserved
49

10 ZION'S COOPERATIVE MERCANTILE INSTITUTION'S SECOND BUILDING
J. Willard Marriott Library
University of Utah
P0507

11 DINWOODEY FURNITURE
J. Willard Marriott Library
University of Utah
P0273

12 CAPSTONE
Library of Congress
157996pu

13 UTE TRIBE
Library of Congress
P0064

14 CHOIR OF MEN
J. Willard Marriott Library
University of Utah
P0001

15 ORIGINAL MORMON PIONEERS
Library of Congress
63677

16 SURVIVORS OF HANDCART COMPANY
Library of Congress
77235

17 HEBER M. WELLS
Used by permission, Utah State Historical Society, all rights reserved
39222001406359

18 STREET PAVING
Used by permission, Utah State Historical Society, all rights reserved
39222000714860

19 VIEW OF CITY AND COUNTY BUILDING
Used by permission, Utah State Historical Society, all rights reserved
39222000711478

20 STAGECOACHES
J. Willard Marriott
Library
University of Utah
p0838n01

22 STREET PAVING
39222000714902

23 PRESIDENT THEODORE
ROOSEVELT
39222001359475

24 STREET PAVING, EAGLE
GATE
39222000714944

25 MEN POSE
J. Willard Marriott
Library
University of Utah
p0838n01_02_03

26 COMMERCIAL STREET
39222000646427

27 A. H. CRABBE
COMPANY
392222000686795

28 COMMERCIAL BLOCK
39222000660428

29 CENTURY PRINTING
COMPANY EMPLOYEES
39222000688916

30 ALTA CLUB
39222000688999

33 VANS IN FRONT OF
HERALD BUILDING
39222000689856

34 ADAMS ELECTRIC
DRILL, SALT LAKE
HARDWARE CO.
39222000690300

35 BICYCLE RIDER
39222000620133

36 PANORAMIC VIEW
39222000723465

37 MAIN STREET
39222000713623

38 BUSTER BROWN CROWD
39222000599964

39 200 SOUTH STREET
39222000711247

40 STREET PAVING, MAIN
STREET AND 200
SOUTH
392220007177962

41 NEWHOUSE BUILDING
39222000603485

42 AUTO, STUDEBAKER
39222000606959

43 PANORAMIC VIEW
39222000723499

44 MAIN STREET AND 300
SOUTH
39222000717921

45 COLUMBIA PHONOGRAPH
COMPANY AUTO
39222000692470

46 MAIN STREET, NORTH
FROM BOSTON BUILDING
39222000711239

47 CASTLE HALL
39222000607486

48 CASTLE HALL
ENTRANCE
39222000607494

49 **BUNGALOW, LYCEUM THEATER**

50 **COLONIAL THEATRE**

51 **STREET PAVING**

52 **AMERICAN LINEN SUPPLY COMPANY WAGONS**

53 **BUNGALOW THEATRE BUILDING**

54 **STREET PAVING**

55 **COLLEGE INN BUILDING**

56 **STREET PAVING**

57 **CADETS AT YOUNG MEN'S CHRISTIAN ASSOCIATION**

58 **LAYING CORNERSTONE OF NEW COMMERCIAL CLUB BUILDING**

59 **BOSTON BUILDING**

60 **OREGON SHORT LINE DEPOT, EXTERIOR**

61 **STREET PAVING, MAIN STREET**

62 **D. J. WATTS BARBER SHOP**

63 **CADETS MARCHING**

64 **CLAYTON-DAYNES MUSIC COMPANY**

65 **AMERICAN HOTEL AND COMMERCIAL STREET**

66 **TAFT AT PARK**

67 **CADETS GUARDING ROAD AT PARK**

68 **EXCHANGE PLACE FROM POST OFFICE**

69 **#11 AND #13 MAIN STREET**

70 **AUTO IN FRONT OF THEATER**

71 **CLIFT HOUSE**

72 **SCENIC VIEW**

73 **BINGHAM**

74 **MAIN STREET**

100 A. H. Crabbe
Used by permission, Utah State Historical Society,
39222000649348

101 University of Utah Baseball Team
Used by permission, Utah State Historical Society,
39222000649827

102 Armour and Company Float
Used by permission, Utah State Historical Society,
39222000651997

103 Campbell Auto Company
Used by permission, Utah State Historical Society,
39222000652011

104 Bertram Motor Supply Company
Used by permission, Utah State Historical Society,
39222000653761

105 Merchants Bank Building
Used by permission, Utah State Historical Society,
39222000654165

106 Bransford Apartment House
Used by permission, Utah State Historical Society,
39222000654421

107 Auerbach Company Store
Used by permission, Utah State Historical Society,
39222000695275

108 Walker Brothers Old Bank Building
Used by permission, Utah State Historical Society,
39222000655477

109 CWM Company
Used by permission, Utah State Historical Society,
39222000658307

110 1200 East Street from South Temple
Used by permission, Utah State Historical Society,
39222000658646

111 Bywater Fire Extinguisher and Supply Store
Used by permission, Utah State Historical Society,
39222000658968

112 Utah State Capitol Construction
Used by permission, Utah State Historical Society,
39222000647383

113 Shipler Studios
Used by permission, Utah State Historical Society,
39222000662887

114 Boyd Park Building
Used by permission, Utah State Historical Society,
39222000663893

115 Crowd
Used by permission, Utah State Historical Society,
39222000725825

116 Utah State Capitol Construction
Used by permission, Utah State Historical Society,
39222000647805

117 East High School Students
Used by permission, Utah State Historical Society,
39222000667092

118 Autos
Used by permission, Utah State Historical Society,
39222000667225

119 Auto in Front of Store
Used by permission, Utah State Historical Society,
39222000668280

120 B. F. Goodrich Rubber Company
Used by permission, Utah State Historical Society,
39222000669999

121 Central Coal and Coke Company
Used by permission, Utah State Historical Society,
39222000670625

122 City and County Building
Used by permission, Utah State Historical Society,
39222000671706

123 Capital Electric Company
Used by permission, Utah State Historical Society,
39222000674619

124 No-Ni-Shee Arch, Main Street
Used by permission, Utah State Historical Society,
39222000674452

125 1300 East Paving Project

126 Swanson Theater Company

127 Kelly-Springfield Truck

128 Public Library

129 Clover Dairy Truck

130 Chevrolet Motor Car Company

131 Botterill

132 C. A. Fowler, Carload of Bicycles in Front of Store

133 Broadway and State Street Intersection

134 200 South and West Temple Intersection

135 Marine Scouts in Auto

136 Oldsmobile at Andersons Tower

139 General Pershing

140 Casino Theatre Lobby

141 State Capitol

142 Harry Pantelakis

143 Circus Side Show

144 Burroughs Adding Machine

145 Rogers Amusement Company

146 Woodrow Wilson

147 Willes Horne Drug Company

148 Fire

149 Beveridge Motor Company

150 Auerbach Company

151 300 South

152 Children at the Thompson Residence

153 Botterill Auto Company

188 HOLY TRINITY GREEK CHURCH
J. Willard Marriott
Library
University of Utah
p0121n01_06_03

189 HARRY TRUMAN
Used by permission, Utah
State Historical Society,
all rights reserved
39222001409254

190 SUGAR HOUSE AREA
Used by permission, Utah
State Historical Society,
all rights reserved
39222000700455

191 AB JENKINS
Used by permission, Utah
State Historical Society,
all rights reserved
39222001353064

192 DAYS OF '47 PARADE
J. Willard Marriott
Library
University of Utah
p0086n47

193 JOHN F. KENNEDY
Used by permission, Utah
State Historical Society,
all rights reserved
39222001354716

194 JOHN F. KENNEDY
Used by permission, Utah
State Historical Society,
all rights reserved
39222001354633

195 CALVIN LEWELLYN RAMPTON
Used by permission, Utah
State Historical Society,
all rights reserved
39222001357891

196 ZIONS FIRST NATIONAL BANK
Used by permission, Utah
State Historical Society,
all rights reserved
157792PU

197 UTAH COMMERCIAL & SAVINGS BANK
Library of Congress
157853PU